STREET CRYPTOGRAPHY
A Quick and Dirty Way to Maintain Your Secret Conspiracy

Christopher Forrest

Copyright 2012 Christopher Forrest
All Rights Reserved
ISBN: 147821015X
ISBN-13: 978-1478210153

Table of Contents

INTRODUCTION..i

PART I
SUBSTITUTION CIPHERS..............................1

Chapter 1
The Caesar Cipher...3

Chapter 2
The Polybius Square.......................................7

Chapter 3
Just For Fun..11

Chapter 4
Vigenere Cipher...17

Chapter 5
Straddling Checkerboard.............................23

PART II
TRANSPOSITION CIPHERS.........................27

Chapter 6
Historic Transposition Ciphers....................29

Chapter 7
Columnar Transposition..............................33

PART III
SECURING A CIPHER..................................39

Chapter 8
Random Number Generation.......................41

Chapter 9
Super Encryption..45

Chapter 10
One Time Pad..47

FINAL THOUGHTS..51

APPENDIX..53

Appendix A
Solutions to Encryptions..................................55

Appendix B
Vic Cipher...59

Appendix C
Checkerboard Variations..................................69

INTRODUCTION

Ok, you have a conspiracy going. You have secret goals and operations going out in all directions. At first, you met face to face with all members of your group, and that worked. Things have changed. You now need a way to secretly deliver a message to someone you won't meet on a regular basis. Congratulations, you picked up the right book.

Before I show you a good way to put together your cipher, I'm going to bore you with the details of why you don't want to use certain other ciphers.

PART I
SUBSTITUTION CIPHERS

CHRISTOPHER FORREST

Chapter 1
The Caesar Cipher

This is, historically, the oldest cipher known to modern man. Its age alone should tell you that it has been beaten, to death, repeatedly. You can even check the New York Times puzzle section to see examples given to be cracked as a game. Long story short, DON'T USE IT.

Now that I've gotten that out of the way, how about we take a look at what the Caesar Cipher actually is?

Julius Caesar was a renowned general, and he needed to get secrets across to his captains and lieutenants. To do this, he used this cool little cipher to thwart interception of his orders, battle plans, and general information by the enemy.

How It Works

He took the Latin alphabet and would shift each letter by a predetermined number. The man in the field would have this number memorized so he could both read the message from his beloved leader and send messages back, without worrying about interception. The translation of such can be shown by Figure 1-1: Caesar Cipher.

Figure 1-1: Caesar Cipher																									
Plaintext	A	B	C	D	E	F	G	H	I	J	K	L	M	N	O	P	Q	R	S	T	U	V	W	X	Y	Z
Ciphertext	D	E	F	G	H	I	J	K	L	M	N	O	P	Q	R	S	T	U	V	W	X	Y	Z	A	B	C

If he wanted to encode the message, "ATTACK AT DAWN", we'd end up with, using Figure 1-1:
DWWDFN DW GDZQ

When the field commander got that message, he could create a table for deciphering the message and clearly read that his commander wanted him to attack at dawn.

Now the field commander has received the message and wants to send a reply. He remembers the shift of 3, and quickly composes a message back to his leader. The message reads:
ZH DUH DW WKH JDWH GR BRX ZDQW WKHLU OHDGHU DOLYH RU GHDG

Caesar reads this and is pleased, so he composes a message back to his field commander that reads:

WKHLU OHDGHU ZLOO PDNH DQ
HAFHOOHQW WURSKB HLWKHU ZDB
WDNH KLP DOLYH LI SRVVLEOH EXW
EULQJ KLV ERGB LI QRW

After the battle, Caesar crowns his captain with a crown of grape leaves and gives him acres of farmland and gold. What do you think happened?

Solutions on Page 55

Crypto analyzing the Caesar Cipher
Now that you can see how the cipher works, let's discuss why you shouldn't use it.

First, there exist only 25 different keys for a Caesar Cipher, considering that the number memorized is the shift. With that in mind, one can feasibly generate 25 copies of your message, each with a different shift, and see which one you used. This would allow an antagonist to know everything you wanted to keep secret from him/her in one tedious afternoon. The only reason it worked for Caesar is: most of his enemies were illiterate, just as most of his soldiers. Were it not for a few literate generals that he campaigned against, as well as competitive legions owned by other Roman generals, he could very well have written his orders in plain text and never needed a cipher.

What if you decide to scramble the alphabet? It doesn't matter. As a simple substitution cipher, it is prone to frequency analysis. This means: if the opposing party has an inkling which language you're using, they can use conventions of that language against you. They may not decipher the first message, but given enough messages, they will have you, and they likely won't be nice enough to tell you so before they lay waste to your plans.

For a detailed introduction to cryptanalysis, I recommend US Army FM 34-40-2, Basic Cryptanalysis.

Chapter 2
The Polybius Square

It is said the god Hermes brought cryptology to the Greeks. A common substitution cipher known to have been widely used by various Greek city-states is the Polybius Square or Polybius Cipher.

This cipher, like the Caesar Cipher, is a simple substitution cipher. Unlike the Caesar Cipher, this one uses a grid of numbers to encode the message. An example is given as Figure 2-1.

Figure 2-1: Polybius Square

	1	2	3	4	5
1	A	B	C	D	E
2	F	G	H	I/J	K
3	L	M	N	O	P
4	Q	R	S	T	U
5	V	W	X	Y	Z

How It Works

If, as before, a general wanted to order one of his captains to attack at dawn, the general would locate the letter on the grid, and then read off the row then column the letter was placed in to find the two digit code for the letter. The encoded message would appear as shown on Figure 2-2.

Figure 2-2: Polybius Encryption

A	T	T	A	C	K	A	T	D	A	W	N
11	44	44	11	13	25	11	44	14	11	52	33

The captain would get this stream of numbers, and would use the square to look up the letters in the message by taking the first number for each pair as the row number, and then he would consider the second number of each pair to be the column number.

Leonidas is rallying his allies against Persia. He composes a message to his friends in Athens:
1334321531154445432124222344531542
5315431144442315423234355431111511
3314434434352324322142343244112524
33221131313421224215151315

His allies in Athens read this message and are emboldened, writing this reply:
5215522431313334443433315443443435
2324322142343244112524332211313134
2122421515131552155224313143443435
2324322142343244112524332211335434
21224215151315114323244 3345233

Solutions on Page 56

As we all know, braggadocio has limited effectiveness in a suicide mission.

Obviously, this is a vastly simplified example, but you see how this could be expanded and used to secure communications.

Why You Shouldn't Rely on This

As I said before in reference to the Caesar Cipher, this is a simple substitution cipher. While the jumble of numbers may appear more secure at first, and, marginally, it is. This will not fool an antagonist for long. The jumble of numbers, each numbered from 1-5, will give this cipher away as some type of grid substitution cipher in minutes. After this fact becomes apparent, a simple frequency analysis will give your message away in days at best, hours at worst, even if the antagonist is working by hand. I've seen one of these ciphers broken in milliseconds with modern computer hardware.

Chapter 3
Just For Fun

OK, we covered a few serious classical substitution ciphers in the previous two chapters, but let us have a little fun. Don't take any of the ciphers in this chapter seriously, and I'll tell you why, but here's a couple that amuse me from time to time.

Pigpen
The pigpen cipher is used by kids worldwide to stump their teachers and amuse themselves in their effort. It is best shown graphically, which I've done in Figure 3-1: Pigpen Cipher.

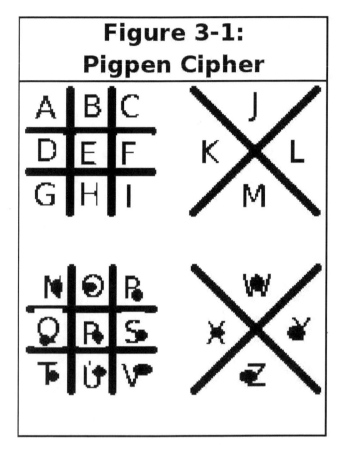

Note that the second half of the alphabet has a dot within the symbol. Each letter of the alphabet is designated by the symbol it is within, for example, the 'A' has a line to the right and a line under, with the two lines intersecting. To denote 'A', you would simply draw the symbol that is denoted.

Why shouldn't you rely on it? Well, it's a simple substitution cipher. Should you use it? Why not? It's fun and wastes time.

FonCode

Have you ever sent a text message on a cellular phone that had a numeric keypad? Well, when you did, did you notice that one would tap on certain numbers as shown on the keypad that coincide with letters? Congratulations, you've used FonCode.

If you're wondering what I'm referring to, see Figure 3-2: Phone Pad. This produces an ambiguous random-looking string of numbers.

Figure 3-2: Phone Pad

1	2 ABC	3 DEF
4 GHI	5 JKL	6 MNO
7 PQRS	8 TUV	9 WXYZ
*	0	#

Here's a sample from a conversation I've seen in action:
Person1: 664 343 968 733 8428 489 43 927 2 86825 7378
Person2: 457 43 927 8682559 37665464 255 6837 968
P1:4 26853 3335 446 8637377464 63 9484 447 3937 27 43
P2:9324 457
P1:76 9428 273 968 36464 8447 9335363
P2:4388464 37865 968

Solutions on Pages 56-57

You can figure out that the text represented here is as mindless as the people using it.

Should you rely on it? Probably not. It's much too vague to count on for anything important. Honestly, many trivial cases have been misinterpreted, leaving one's texts taking a context that one never intended. Also, anyone who has a cellular phone has a key to your code, so security is nonexistent.

ROT13
This is simply Caesar with a rotation of 13.

Should you know this? If you participate in Geek culture, the answer is definitely, Yes! This is used in many Internet forums, on IRC channels, newsgroups, etc. It isn't used to add security, but to add one step to deciphering the text. In other words, you will not read something that is encoded with ROT13 unless you want to read it.

What remotely useable cipher would be presented in this book without samples? Sir, that sounds like a PEBKAC error (CEBOYRZ RKVFGF ORGJRRA XRLOBNEQ NAQ PUNVE). It's pretty serious.
We did what any responsible Netizen would do in the circumstance (SNC).
I have a hot date (jvgu lbhe zbz) so let me know how that game went, OK?
That guy isn't 1337. ohg uvf zbz ubjrire vf n frevbhf zvys

Solutions on Page 57

Now that we've had a little fun, let's talk about one cipher that provides a little real security to your messages.

Chapter 4
Vigenere Cipher

In previous chapters, I showed you ciphers of recreational and historical interest, and this cipher is no exception, but this cipher will definitely protect your text from a passing observer. Make no mistakes; I do not pretend that this cipher will keep a dedicated observer from cracking your code, but this will keep all away but the hobbyist and the determined.

The Vigenere Cipher is best described as many Caesar shift ciphers combined at once. The timing of the shifts is usually determined by a keyword, and the user of a Vigenere Cipher usually carries on him a cipher wheel or a Vigenere Square.

How It Works

For any group to use the Vigenere Cipher, first, all involved must agree on a key to use. This key is typically one easy to remember word. For the sake of simplicity, let's say that the group is a couple of teens wanting to keep their 'friends' from reading their communications. Let's say for the same reason the two teens are named Bob and Sally and the two have agreed on the key 'CIPHER' to protect their messages.

Figure 4-1: Vigenere Square

	A	B	C	D	E	F	G	H	I	J	K	L	M	N	O	P	Q	R	S	T	U	V	W	X	Y	Z
A	A	B	C	D	E	F	G	H	I	J	K	L	M	N	O	P	Q	R	S	T	U	V	W	X	Y	Z
B	B	C	D	E	F	G	H	I	J	K	L	M	N	O	P	Q	R	S	T	U	V	W	X	Y	Z	A
C	C	D	E	F	G	H	I	J	K	L	M	N	O	P	Q	R	S	T	U	V	W	X	Y	Z	A	B
D	D	E	F	G	H	I	J	K	L	M	N	O	P	Q	R	S	T	U	V	W	X	Y	Z	A	B	C
E	E	F	G	H	I	J	K	L	M	N	O	P	Q	R	S	T	U	V	W	X	Y	Z	A	B	C	D
F	F	G	H	I	J	K	L	M	N	O	P	Q	R	S	T	U	V	W	X	Y	Z	A	B	C	D	E
G	G	H	I	J	K	L	M	N	O	P	Q	R	S	T	U	V	W	X	Y	Z	A	B	C	D	E	F
H	H	I	J	K	L	M	N	O	P	Q	R	S	T	U	V	W	X	Y	Z	A	B	C	D	E	F	G
I	I	J	K	L	M	N	O	P	Q	R	S	T	U	V	W	X	Y	Z	A	B	C	D	E	F	G	H
J	J	K	L	M	N	O	P	Q	R	S	T	U	V	W	X	Y	Z	A	B	C	D	E	F	G	H	I
K	K	L	M	N	O	P	Q	R	S	T	U	V	W	X	Y	Z	A	B	C	D	E	F	G	H	I	J
L	L	M	N	O	P	Q	R	S	T	U	V	W	X	Y	Z	A	B	C	D	E	F	G	H	I	J	K
M	M	N	O	P	Q	R	S	T	U	V	W	X	Y	Z	A	B	C	D	E	F	G	H	I	J	K	L
N	N	O	P	Q	R	S	T	U	V	W	X	Y	Z	A	B	C	D	E	F	G	H	I	J	K	L	M
O	O	P	Q	R	S	T	U	V	W	X	Y	Z	A	B	C	D	E	F	G	H	I	J	K	L	M	N
P	P	Q	R	S	T	U	V	W	X	Y	Z	A	B	C	D	E	F	G	H	I	J	K	L	M	N	O
Q	Q	R	S	T	U	V	W	X	Y	Z	A	B	C	D	E	F	G	H	I	J	K	L	M	N	O	P
R	R	S	T	U	V	W	X	Y	Z	A	B	C	D	E	F	G	H	I	J	K	L	M	N	O	P	Q
S	S	T	U	V	W	X	Y	Z	A	B	C	D	E	F	G	H	I	J	K	L	M	N	O	P	Q	R
T	T	U	V	W	X	Y	Z	A	B	C	D	E	F	G	H	I	J	K	L	M	N	O	P	Q	R	S
U	U	V	W	X	Y	Z	A	B	C	D	E	F	G	H	I	J	K	L	M	N	O	P	Q	R	S	T
V	V	W	X	Y	Z	A	B	C	D	E	F	G	H	I	J	K	L	M	N	O	P	Q	R	S	T	U
W	W	X	Y	Z	A	B	C	D	E	F	G	H	I	J	K	L	M	N	O	P	Q	R	S	T	U	V
X	X	Y	Z	A	B	C	D	E	F	G	H	I	J	K	L	M	N	O	P	Q	R	S	T	U	V	W
Y	Y	Z	A	B	C	D	E	F	G	H	I	J	K	L	M	N	O	P	Q	R	S	T	U	V	W	X
Z	Z	A	B	C	D	E	F	G	H	I	J	K	L	M	N	O	P	Q	R	S	T	U	V	W	X	Y

Bob wants to ask Sally out to a movie, but doesn't want his jock friends to laugh at him for dating the nerdy girl. He first composes a short message: "Would you like to go out to the movies Friday night?" He pulls out his Vigenere Square (Figure 4-1) and applies the cipher, like so:
The first letter of the key is 'C', so the first letter of the message coincides to the letter where column 'C' meets row 'W', which is 'Y'. The second letter of the key is 'I', and the second letter of the message is 'O', so he would find where column 'I' and row 'O' intersect, which is 'W'. Continuing for the first six characters, he has the message: "YWJSH P". Now, what to do? He's worked through the key, so he starts over with 'C' of the key, and continues until he encodes all of his message, giving: "YWJSH PQC APOV VW VV SLV BD ALV OWKPIJ HZXKEP PQVOX".

Let's make the assumption, however unlikely, that someone in his peer group is intelligent enough to start crypto analyzing it. Bob, being clever, removes any information, like spaces, that would aid such analysis, leaving a dead string of letters and no clue which cipher, the length of the key, and especially not the key.

Anyways, let's assume that Bob gets the message to Sally. Sally uses her copy of a Vigenere Square with the key 'CIPHER' as such:

Sally starts with the letter 'C' of the key, and reads across the row until she finds the first letter of the message, 'Y', and finds that it is in column designated for the letter 'W'. She uses the second letter of the key, 'I' as the row for the second letter of the message, and so on, until she deciphers the message. Soon enough, she ends up with the plaintext:
"WOULDYOULIKETOGOOUTTOTHEMOVIESFRIDAYNIGHT"

Sally is flattered at the offer, but is skeptical of his intentions. She wants an assurance that his intentions are genuine, so she decides to forgo the movie night in favor of dinner with her family. She composes the message:
"NO, BUT YOU CAN COME OVER FOR DINNER WITH MY FAMILY"

Using the key and the Vigenere Square to encrypt, this gives:
"PWQBXPQCRARTQUTVZVTNDYHZPVTYAZVPBFJROQAF".

Bob receives and decrypts Sally's reply and decides not to come to dinner, confirming Sally's suspicion. She changes her working key and teaches other silly boys how to use ciphers.

Why You Shouldn't Rely On This

To be honest, this cipher is pretty secure. It's breakable, but with modifications, it can be an extremely difficult endeavor. For messages that aren't of high priority or if your messages aren't necessarily that secret to begin with, this cipher is perfectly acceptable. If someone wanted to crack your message, first one would need to assume it was Vigenere, and then one would look for repeating patterns within the cipher text to guess the length of the key. Once one has a guess for the length of the key, one would proceed to crack it as multiple Caesar ciphers. If you use this cipher, don't assume the message secret from all, and change your key frequently.

Chapter 5
Straddling Checkerboard

In the previous chapter, I showed you a cipher known as the Vigenere. While that cipher is rather good, it only leaves room for alphabetic characters. While there is nothing particularly wrong with that, many of us need to encode numbers and symbols in messages for them to be understood. This is where a straddling checkerboard comes in.

What Is It?
The straddling checkerboard is a grid used to encode data. Unlike ASCII or UTF, it isn't standardized. This means you can make your own system that meets all your needs, but is largely unused and unaccounted-for outside of your group.

An extremely simple example of a straddling checkerboard is the one used in the Vic cipher, given in Figure 5-1, thanks to Dirk Rijmenant. More examples will be available in the Appendix.

Figure 5-1: Vic Checkerboard

	0	1	2	3	4	5	6	7	8	9
	A	E	I	N	O	R	S	T		
8	B	C	D	F	G	H	J	K	L	M
9	P	Q	U	V	W	X	Y	Z	SPC	L/F

Yeah, I know that that particular checkerboard is extremely basic, only giving you letters and numbers, but let's assume for a moment that this checkerboard is all we need. Let's say you want to send a message using this checkerboard. For letters on the top row, one would only use one digit for the code for that character. For letters in other rows, one would take the number designated by the row as the first digit in a two digit code. For numbers, one would first give the code for L/F(Letters to figures) as a shifting character, repeat the numbers to show the receiver that the numbers aren't an error, then finish with the code for L/F. Using Figure 5-1, the message: "Meet me at the docks at 1800" would look like this:
89 1 1 7 98 89 1 98 0 7 98 7 85 1 98 82 4 81 87 6 98 0 7 98 99 111 888 000 000 99

Now to remove clues, one would format it before sending it, like so:
89117 98891 98079 87851 98824 81876 98079 89911 18880 00000 99

Do you have to put spaces in it? No. Do you need to make the tokens of cipher text five characters long? No. I've just found that it's easier to copy and verify as five character tokens. For your use, do what you like.

Of course this is not the only straddling checkerboard. Intelligence agencies have used multiple. Further, there's absolutely no reason you can't make your own. As a matter of fact, I encourage it.

Why You Shouldn't Rely On This
Well, in its current form, it's a simple substitution cipher, so instead of "Don't rely on this", I would say "Don't rely on this alone as your cipher". This cipher works well when combined with other ciphers for your personal cipher, as I'll show you later in this text.

PART II
TRANSPOSITION CIPHERS

Chapter 6
Historic Transposition Ciphers

Here I'll briefly discuss a few transposition ciphers used throughout the ages from the ancient Spartans to the German army.

Spartan Scytale
It remains unclear whether the scytale was a method of encryption or a method of authentication, but the scytale was used extensively by the Spartans to get messages to the captains in the field.

What Is It?

The scytale itself was just a pole of predetermined size and shape, upon which a leather belt was wrapped. The message was written across the belt, making for a field expedient cipher. To read the message, one would wrap the belt around an identical scytale and read off the message sent. This was cracked by the Macedonians, the Persians, the Romans, and any other army or insurgent group who had the cojones to come up against the Spartans. In other words, it wasn't very secure.

Grille Ciphers

I'm not going to go through and iterate each and every grille cipher that came down the pipe. Let's make it simple: It was used often, by many, including the German army. It involves cutting a proprietary "grid" from metal or paper, then writing your message within the grid before filling the spaces with trash information to confuse a cryptanalyst. It usually didn't work, considering that most of these Grille ciphers called for writing complete words of the message in place, in plaintext.

There exist other methods of transposition, but I'm personally more interested in showing you a couple that have been used more recently in military ciphers.

Chapter 7
Columnar
Transposition

I skipped a lot regarding transposition in favor of jumping straight to the meat of the matter, a columnar transposition. It has been used by the British, the Soviets, and various European intelligence agencies. I personally consider it a vital portion of one's personal cipher.

What Is It?

Well, a columnar transposition is, just that, a shuffle of text by columns. Say you have a group who discuss scandalous things regarding members of the public. You've decided to use a columnar transposition to keep your messages out of public purview, and have agreed on the key "scandals" as your key. One of your confederates wants to express his opinion, so he puts together his message:

"I caught the mayor's wife with a man half her age at Club Nostalgia. Can't she keep her hands to herself?"

and, using the key is laid out in Figure 7-1.

Figure 7-1
Simple Transposition

S	C	A	N	D	A	L	S
I	C	A	U	G	H	T	T
H	E	M	A	Y	O	R	S
W	I	F	E	W	I	T	H
A	M	A	N	H	A	L	F
H	E	R	A	G	E	A	T
C	L	U	B	N	O	S	T
A	L	G	I	A	C	A	N
T	S	H	E	K	E	E	P
H	E	R	H	A	N	D	S
T	O	H	E	R	S	E	L
F							

One would use the key to determine which column to read off first. I would recommend going alphabetically, and after, left to right. In the above, the earliest letter, alphabetically, in the key is 'A', but that letter occurs twice, so we would read the third column down first, and we'd end up with:
AMFARUGHRH HOIAEOCENS CEIMELLSEO GYWHGNAKAR TRTLASAEDE UAENABIEHE IHWAHCATHTF TSHFTTNPSL

In case someone assumed it to be a transposition, he removed the spaces, and then tokenized the text, as:
AMFAR-UGHRH-HOIAE-OCENS-CEIME-LLSEO-GYWHG-NAKAR-TRTLA-SAEDE-UAENA-BIEHE-IHWAH-CATHT-FTSHF-TTNPS-L

To spread his opinion, he published this text in the personals section of a local newspaper. Most won't know what he said, but those in the know will know, clearly what he said.

Why You Shouldn't Rely On This
First things first, the message is scrambled, but there is no substitution involved, so if one was to guess it was a simple transposition, they could take guesses at the length and in a matter of hours come up with the plaintext. But also keep in mind, this is a vastly simplified version of what computers do in "block ciphers" to encrypt your data. Combine several iterations of this with another method, say Vigenere or straddling checkerboard, and you have yourself a pretty good cipher.

Can We Make It Better?
Sure can! Let's assume the above, but instead of a simple columnar transposition, we do a disrupted transposition. I like examples, so Figure 7-2.

Figure 7-2
Disrupted Transposition

S	C	A	N	D	A	L	S
I	C	A					
U	G	H	T	T	H		
E	M						
A	Y	O	R	S			
W	I	F	E	W	I	T	
H	A	M	A				
N							
H	A	L	F	H	E	R	A
G	E	A					
T	C	L	U	B	N		
O	S						
T	A	L	G	I			
A	C	A	N	T	S	H	
E	K	E					
E							
P	H	E	R	H	A	N	D
S	T	O					
H	E	R	S	E	L		
F							

Using such, you get:
AHOFMLALLAEEOR-HIENSAL-
CGMYIAAECSACKHTE-TSWHBITHE-TRHN-
TREAFUGNRS-IUEAWHNHGTOTAEEPSHF-
AD

And when you tokenize it:
AHOFM-LALLA-EEORH-IENSA-LCGMY-IAAEC-SACKH-TETSW-HBITH-ETRHN-TREAF-UGNRS-IUEAW-HNHGT-OTAEE-PSHFA-D

This provides a confusing and greatly scrambled message. It's great for keeping someone from crypto analyzing the cipher text. It still won't keep out a determined antagonist, but it goes far in that regard, much like the Vigenere cipher does.

PART III
SECURING A CIPHER

Chapter 8
Random Number Generation

For one to have a truly secure cipher, one needs to apply random or pseudorandom numbers to any algorithm. In this chapter, I plan to explore a few methods of generating your random or pseudorandom numbers.

Chain Addition
This is used in the Vic cipher, as well as a few other pencil-paper ciphers out on the web. It works like this: one takes their passphrase, performs an operation or few on it, and then begins a lagged Fibonacci process on the string.

You know I love examples by now, so take a look at Figure 8-1. In this figure, I took a date: 70476(Independence Day in the US), and 91101(the day New York was struck in a suicide attack on the World Trade Center). The first line are the dates themselves, and then I went through the numbers giving the lowest number, 1, the lower values, and moving up to 0, which is equivalent to 10 in this example. From there, we add the number to the number next to it, neglecting carries, and put the result in the row below, In doing so, I generated 50 "random" digits.

Figure 8-1
Chain Addition

7	0	4	7	6	9	1	1	0	1
6	9	4	7	5	8	1	2	0	3
5	3	1	2	3	9	3	2	3	8
8	4	3	5	2	2	5	5	1	6
2	7	8	7	4	7	0	6	7	8
9	5	5	1	1	7	6	3	5	7
4	0	6	2	8	3	9	8	2	1

Center Squares
This is the method used by mainframe computers from the 70's to generate "random" numbers. The seed will be squared, and the middle digits of the number (same length as seed) will be taken as part of the stream of random numbers. Those middle digits will seed back into the function to generate more digits. I recommend one use a table of squares for this method. Also note: this method is limited by the length of seed. If you only put a three digit number as original seed, there can exist, at most, 1000 iterations of the function before it begins to repeat.

Center Roots
Think center squares in reverse. This produces a long decimal value that can be fed as a string of random-looking digits, and the same limitations apply.

Coins and Dice

Unlike the above, these are truly random. The problem exists: if it's truly random, how can one know that it will be generated identically on both sides? The answer: it won't be. The chances of both sender and receiver generating same random sequence approaches 0 faster than your chances of winning a lottery by going fishing. A true random number generation is great for producing an encryption that can't be cracked, under certain circumstances, but for the other end to be able to decrypt, both ends must have the same list of numbers and agree on how to encrypt/decrypt the message.

Chapter 9
Super Encryption

In previous chapters, I showed you a few ciphers, how they worked, and gave a hint about possible weakness. "Ok, we get it, but how do you make up for the weaknesses?" you may be asking. Well, it's rather simple: you implement a technique called super encryption to attempt to make up for shortcomings in a cipher.

What Is It?

Super encryption is simply the use of multiple ciphers, usually in multiple steps, as a singular encryption scheme. Say, for example, we had the Vigenere Cipher as our first step. You think, "Well, that's great." Yes, it is, but what if you added a columnar transposition to the Vigenere? This would make things more difficult to crack. Let's say, for example, that you had a custom straddling checkerboard, you used a pair of columnar transpositions, one simple and another disrupted. That is much more difficult than a Vigenere, by any measure, to crack. As a matter of fact, this very scheme was used by the Soviets to send messages to their operatives in the United States during the 1950's.

Should You Rely On This?

Well, this isn't an encryption cipher as it is combining ciphers into an algorithm, so, yes, you should rely on this, with a caveat: Test test test this to verify security.

Chapter 10
One Time Pad

Ok, I promised to show you a cipher that was virtually unbreakable, and here it is. With proper key security and proper key usage, this cipher is mathematically unbreakable.

What Is It?

One time pad is more a keying scheme than a cipher in itself. The pad is a set of random characters, be they decimal, alphabetical, hexadecimal, etc. used to encipher a message. To keep the key secure, simply tear the sheet or sheets used to encode the message from the pad and destroy. By destroy, I don't mean throw away. I don't mean flush down the toilet. I personally recommend you shred the key used, then put the shreddings in an oven preheated to 550 degrees Fahrenheit, then mix the ashes with your cigarette ashes and butts, then flush the whole mess. Don't smoke? Well, if you're dealing with information so sensitive that you're using a one time pad, you may want to start. You likely won't live to get lung cancer anyways. If you're needing such an extreme level of security to use one time pad, I'd also advise you doing the same to the paper used to encode the message, the plaintext message, and any plaintext messages you have received. If your security needs are this great, you can't be too careful. If your pad is discovered, I personally recommend you notify your confederates as soon as you can safely do so. A compromised pad is dangerous, should you be needing one in the first place. You can implement a one time pad in multiple ways. If you use a decimal one time pad, you will need to agree to a system to encode your entire message by in base 10 numbers, preferably of fixed length or via a straddling checkerboard. If you use an alphabetic pad, you can simply use the letters as Caesar shifts ala the Vigenere square. If you use a hexadecimal pad, it's rather simple to use any of many computer-based character tables as your initial step to encode and encrypt your message. The one time pad really does simplify the process.

You're probably thinking, "Yeah, that's great, but what's wrong with it?" Plenty. First, you must have a trusted way of distributing the pad to the right people. Second, you must train those people to use it. Finally, each person with a copy of the pad must successfully guard it. There are workarounds, of course, but each workaround has its own problems. I'd strongly recommend that if you use this system, keep it to high level communications or hire someone like myself to manage your cryptography and field cryptology. You'll thank me for this advice, should you follow it.

In conclusion, One Time Pad may be theoretically unbreakable, but it is extremely difficult to implement and secure. Use it only if you must.

FINAL THOUGHTS

Before you send me angry emails saying, "You didn't go in depth about cryptanalysis!", "Why didn't you give me more examples?", "Your book glosses over everything and oversimplifies", or something similar, please know that this is a layman's introduction and should be treated as such. I intended to give you a few ideas to start with and watch you go from there. Could I have given more historical ciphers? Sure. I also could have written a 1000 page volume on historical cryptography. Could I have given digital ciphers? Yeah, but this is for street use, away from a computer when you don't trust your phone (It's probably being tracked, so you pull the battery.) Could I have gone more in depth? Sure, but then why would you buy my next book? Ok, I'm just kidding on the last one. I went to the depth I felt I must to demonstrate the concept clearly, and then let your imagination take it from there.

APPENDIX

Appendix A
Solutions to Encryptions

Chapter 1

ZH DUH DW WKH JDWH GR BRX ZDQW
WKHLU OHDGHU DOLYH RU GHDG
WE ARE AT THE GATE DO YOU WANT
THEIR LEADER ALIVE OR DEAD

WKHLU OHDGHU ZLOO PDNH DQ
HAFHOOHQW WURSKB HLWKHU ZDB
WDNH KLP DOLYH LI SRVVLEOH EXW
EULQJ KLV ERGB LI QRW
THEIR LEADER WILL MAKE AN EXCELLENT
TROPHY EITHER WAY TAKE HIM ALIVE IF
POSSIBLE BUT BRING HIS BODY IF NOT

Chapter 2

1334321531154445432124222344531542
5315431144442315423234355431111511
3314434434352324322142343244112524
332211313134212242151513 15
COME LET US FIGHT XERXES AT
THERMOPYLAE AND STOP HIM FROM
TAKING ALL OF GREECE

5215522431313334443433315443443435
2324322142343244112524332211313134
2122421515131552155224313143443435
2324322142343244112524332211335434
21224215151315114323244334 5233
WE WILL NOT ONLY STOP HIM FROM
TAKING ALL OF GREECE WE WILL STOP
HIM FROM TAKING ANY OF GREECE AS HIS
OWN

Chapter 3

Person1: 664 343 968 733 8428 489 43
927 2 86825 7378
OMG DID YOU SEE THAT GUY HE WAS A
TOTAL PERV

Person2: 457 43 927 8682559 37665464
255 6837 968
IKR HE WAS TOTALLY DROOLING ALL OVER
YOU

P1:4 26854 3335 446 8637377464 63
9484 447 3937 27 43
I COULD FEEL HIM UNDRESSING ME WITH
HIS EYES AS IF

P2:9324 457
YEAH IKR

P1:76 9428 273 968 36464 8447 9335363
SO WHAT ARE YOU DOING THIS WEEKEND

P2:4388464 37865 968
GETTING DRUNK YOU

Sir, that sounds like a PEBKAC error
(CEBOYRZ RKVFGF ORGJRRA XRLOBNEQ
NAQ PUNVE). It's pretty serious.
PROBLEM EXISTS BETWEEN KEYBOARD
AND CHAIR

We did what any responsible Netizen
would do in the circumstance (SNC).
FAP

I have a hot date (jvgu lbhe zbz) so let me
know how that game went, OK?
with your mom

That guy isn't 1337. ohg uvf zbz ubjrire vf
n frevbhf zvys
but his mom however is a serious milf

Appendix B
Vic Cipher

First, I want to thank John Savard for providing such an excellent description of the Vic cipher. I couldn't think of a better way to explain the cipher, so this particular appendix is just a copy of his explanation on his website: http://www.quadibloc.com. The URL for the original page: http://www.quadibloc.com/crypto/pp1324.htm.

The VIC Cipher

The VIC cipher is an intricate cipher issued by the Soviet Union to at least one of its spies. It is of interest because it seems highly secure, despite being a pencil-and-paper cipher. It was the cipher in which a message was written which was found on a piece of microfilm inside a hollowed-out nickel by a newspaper boy in 1953. The workings of this cipher were explained by Hayhaynen to FBI agents shortly after his defection to the United States in 1957.

David Kahn described that cipher briefly in an article in Scientific American, and in full detail in a talk at the 1960 annual convention of the American Cryptogram Association which was later reprinted in his book Kahn on Codes.

The VIC cipher, which I will demonstrate here adapted to the sending of English-language messages, begins with an involved procedure to produce ten pseudorandom digits. The agent must have memorized six digits (which were in the form of a date), and the first 20 letters of a key phrase (which was the beginning of a popular song) and must think of five random digits for use as a message indicator.

Let the date be July 4, 1776, to give the digits 741776. (Actually, the Russians used their customary form of dates, with the month second.) And let the random indicator group be 77651.

The first step is to perform digit by digit subtraction (without carries) of the first five digits of the date from the indicator group:

```
     77651
(-)  74177
    ------
     03584
```

The second step is to take the 20-letter keyphrase, and turn it into 20 digits by dividing it into two halves, and within each half, assigning 1 to the letter earliest in the alphabet, and so on, treating 0 as the last number, and assigning digits in order to identical letters. Thus, if our keyphrase is "I dream of Jeannie with t", that step proceeds:

```
I D R E A M O F J E   A N N I E W I T H T
6 2 0 3 1 8 9 5 7 4   1 6 7 4 2 0 5 8 3 9
```

The result of the first step is then expanded to ten digits through a process called chain addition. This is a decimal analog of the way a linear-feedback shift register works: starting with a group of a certain number of digits (in this case five, and later we will do the same thing with a group of ten digits), add the first two digits in the group together, take only the last digit of the result and append it to the end of the group, then ignore the first digit, and repeat the process.

The 10 digit result is then added, digit by digit, ignoring carries, to the first 10 digits produced from the keyphrase to produce a ten-digit result, as follows:

```
      6 2 0 3 1 8 9 5 7 4
(+)   0 3 5 8 4 3 8 3 2 7
    ----------------------
      6 5 5 1 5 1 7 8 9 1
```

And these 10 digits are then encoded by encoding 1 as the first of the 10 digits produced from the second half of the keyphrase, 2 as the second, up to 0 as the tenth.

```
using code: 1 2 3 4 5 6 7 8 9 0
            1 6 7 4 2 0 5 8 3 9
            6 5 5 1 5 1 7 8 9 1
becomes     0 2 2 1 2 1 5 8 3 1
```

This ten digit number is used by chain addition to generate 50 pseudorandom digits for use in encipherment:

```
0 2 2 1 2 1 5 8 3 1
---------------------
2 4 3 3 3 6 3 1 4 3
6 7 6 6 9 9 4 5 7 9
3 3 2 5 8 3 9 2 6 2
6 5 7 3 1 2 1 8 8 8
1 2 0 4 3 3 9 6 6 9
```

The last row of these digits (which will still be used again) is used like the letters in a keyword for transposition to produce a permutation of the digits 1 through 9 (with 0 last again):

```
1 2 0 4 3 3 9 6 6 9
---------------------
1 2 0 5 3 4 8 6 7 9
```

and those digits are used as the top row of numbers for a straddling checkerboard:

```
  1 2   0 5 3 4 8 6 7 9
  ---------------------
  A T   O N E   S I R
  ---------------------
0 B C D F G H J K L M
8 P Q U V W X Y Z . /
```

One detail omitted is that the checkerboard actually used had the letters in the bottom part written in vertical columns with some columns left until the end. That doesn't work as well in an English example, as there are only two left-over spaces after the alphabet.

With the straddling checkerboard in place, we can begin enciphering a message.

Let our message be:
We are pleased to hear of your success in establishing your false identity. You will be sent some money to cover expenses within a month.

Converting this to numbers, we proceed:

```
W EAREP L EASED TOH EAROF Y OU RSU C C ESSINESTAB L ISH ING
83419481074164002504419505885809680020246673462101077604730 3
Y OU RF AL SEID ENTITY Y OU W IL L B ESENTSOM EM ONEY TOC O
88580905107647004327288885808370707014643265094095348825025
V EREX P ENSESW ITH INAM ONTH
85494848143646837204731095320 4
```

For the sake of our example, we will give our agent a small personal number of 8. This number is used to work out the widths of the two transposition tableaux used to transpose the numbers obtained above. The last two unequal digits, which in this case are the last two digits (6 and 9) of the last row of the 50 numbers generated above, are added to the personal number with the result that the two transpositions will involve 8+6, or 14, and 8+9, or 17, columns respectively.

The keys for those two transpositions are taken by reading out the 50 numbers by columns, using the 10 digits used to generate them as a transposition key. Again, 0 is last, so given the table above:

```
0 2 2 1 2 1 5 8 3 1
---------------------
2 4 3 3 3 6 3 1 4 3
6 7 6 6 9 9 4 5 7 9
3 3 2 5 8 3 9 2 6 2
6 5 7 3 1 2 1 8 8 8
1 2 0 4 3 3 9 6 6 9
```

we read out the digits in order:
36534 69323 39289 47352 36270 39813 4

stopping when we have the 31 digits we need.

Our first transposition uses the first 14 digits as the key of a conventional simple columnar transposition:

```
36534693233928
--------------
83419481074164
00250441950588
58096800202466
73462101077604
73038858090510
76470043272888
85808370707014
64326509409534
88250258549484
81436468372047
3109532049
```

Since our message consisted of ten rows of 14 digits, plus one extra row of 9 digits, it is 149 digits long. At this initial stage, one null digit is appended to the message, making it 150 digits long, so that it will fill a whole number of 5-digit groups.

Thus, with the null digit added, it gives us the intermediate form of the message:
   09200274534 6860181384 80577786883 15963702539 11018309880
   75079700479 4027027992 90628086065 42040483240 30833654811
   44818035243 4864084447 84005470562 1546580540

The fact that our message is 150 digits long was important to note, since the next step in the encipherment, although it is also a columnar transposition, includes an extra complexity to make the transposition irregular, and so it is necessary to lay out in advance the space that will be used in that transposition.

The remaining 17 digits of the 31 we read out above, 9 47352 36270 39813 4, are the key for this second transposition. The numbers, in addition to indicating the order in which the columns are to be read out, indicate where triangular areas start which will be filled in last.

The first triangular area starts at the top of the column which will be read out first, and extends to the end of the first row. It continues in the next row, starting one column later, and so on until it includes only the digit in the last column. Then, after one space, the second triangular area starts, this time in the column which will be read out second.

Since we know that our message is 150 digits long, we know that it will fill 8 rows of 17 digits, with 14 digits in the final row. This lets us fill in the transposition block, first avoiding the triangular areas:

```
94735236270398134
-----------------
09200274534686
018138480577786
8831596370253911
01830988075079700
47940
270279
9290628
08606542
040483240
```

and then with them filled in as well:

```
94735236270398134
-----------------
09200274534686308
01813848057778633
88315963702539116
01830988075079700
47940548114481803
27027952434864084
92906284478400547
08606542056215465
04048324080540
```

from which the fully encrypted message can be read out:
36178054 289959253 507014400
011342004 746845842 675048425
03100846 918177284 83603475
035007668 483882424 283890960
350713758 689914050 008042900
873786014 472544860

The last digit, 6, in the date shows that the indicator group is to be inserted in the final message as the sixth group from the end, so the message in the form in which it will be transmitted becomes:
36178 05428 99592 53507 01440 00113
42004 74684 58426 75048
42503 10084 69181 77284 83603 47503
50076 68483 88242 42838
90960 35071 37586 89914 05000 77651
80429 00873 78601 44725
44860

Appendix C
Checkerboard Variations

I'd like to thank Dirk Rijmenants for providing me with the page that I'll blatantly paste as this appendix. The original URL for the page is http://users.telenet.be/d.rijmenants/en/table.htm. Note: his formatting was lost in formatting this as a book, so you may see references to colors or hyperlinks that don't exist in this version.

This page contains some variations of the straddling checkerboard, a system to convert text into digits. This conversion is not a type of encryption and offers absolutely no cryptographic protection whatsoever! The conversion only prepares the plain text for the actual encryption process. There are many different methods to convert text into numbers. Some are suitable for text only, others enable the use of other characters. Simple systems are easy to remember but more complex systems have more possibilities. We will demonstrate several different conversion tables, each of them with its own characteristics and advantages. For practical reasons, the conversion tables are named after the number of characters they support (CT-xx). These are no official or existing names. Please visit the one-time pad and manual one-time pads pages for more information.

The first table is the easiest one. The alphabet is numbered A = 01 trough Z = 26 and 00 for a space. L/F 88 (letters/figures) is used just before and after figures and these figures are converted into themselves, written three times to exclude errors (assigning two-digit values to numbers is not advicable as these are prone to single-digit errors). CODE 99 is an optional codebook prefix, followed by a codebook prefix for fixed length code. The second row, from 30 onwards, is optional. If you don't use any optional characters, you can use an "X" as a decimal point and a "Y" as a comma within figures mode.

SPC	A	B	C	D	E	F	G	H	I	J	K	L	M	N	O	P	Q	R	S	T	U	V	W	X	Y	Z	L/F	CODE
00	01	02	03	04	05	06	07	08	09	10	11	12	13	14	15	16	17	18	19	20	21	22	23	24	25	26	88	99
(.)	(,)	(:)	(')	(")	(	)	?	!	%	Optional characters...																		
30	31	32	33	34	35	36	37	38	39	40 ...																		

This approach has the advantage of easy use in the field and doesn't require the help of a complex or hard to remember conversion table. Of course, this method can be expanded with other characters, special tokens, upper and lower case letters, or adapted for any other language. A downside is that a message will be longer due to the two-digit values for all letters. From the security point of view there is no difference with the other conversion systems, described further on, if correctly encrypted with one-time pad. This method is very suitable for small messages and unexperienced personnel.

An example conversion:
M E E T - M E - A T   1 0 3 0 H R
13 04 04 20 00 13 04 00 01 20 88 111 000 333 000 88 08 18

In groups:
13040 42000 13040 00120 88111 00033 30008 80818

A second method is to use a straddling checkerboard. The most frequently used letters are converted into one-digit values. All other letters, the space and letters/figures have two-digit values. This reduces the size of the message considerably (+/- 150% of the plaintext against >200% for the previous method). In a straddling checkerboard, the first row contains the single digit characters and is numbered 0 to 7. In the example below we use the eight most frequent English letters SENORITA. The second and third rows contain the remaining letters, L/F 98 and SPACE 99. L/F is used just before and after figures and the figures are converted into themselves, written three times to exclude errors. Use an "X" as a decimal point and a "Y" as a comma within figures mode. Other characters can be replaced by rare combinations, for instance, XX for full stop, ZZ for a slant, YY as optional codebook prefix.

The original checkerboard works with columns and rows. If a letter is found in the first row, we take the digit of the column. If the letters is found in the second or third row we take the digit of that row and the digit of that column (R = 4, H = 85, P = 90 etc).

```
|0 1 2 3 4 5 6 7 8 9
+-------------------------------
|S E N O R I T A
8| B C D F G H J K L M
9| P Q U V W X Y Z lf spc
```

Presented in a practical table:

S	E	N	O	R	I	T	A		
0	1	2	3	4	5	6	7		
B	C	D	F	G	H	J	K	L	M
80	81	82	83	84	85	86	87	88	89
P	Q	U	V	W	X	Y	Z	L/F	SPC
90	91	92	93	94	95	96	97	98	99

An example conversion:
```
M E E T - M E - A T   1 0 3 0
H R
 89 1 1 6  99 89 1  99 7  6  98 111 000
333 000 98 85 4
```

In groups:
89116 99891 99769 81110 00333 00098 854

Note that even this very small text is already seven digits smaller than the previous simple method!

When decrypting a message, how do we know if we have to read a single-digit or double-digit character? You simply look at the next digit to read. If it starts with 0 through 7, you have a single-digit value. If it starts with 8 or 9, you have a two-digit value and there's one more digit to read for this particular character.

The order of the characters can be changed to any desired combination. Some other anagrams for the letters "SENORITA" are "A-NOTE-SIR", "NATO-RISE-", "RAT-NOISE-", or "NO-TEA-SIR". Of course, the letters can be replaced by the most frequent letters of another language. In such case, the second and third rows are again filled with the remaining characters. The position of the two blank fields in the top row can also be changed. For instance, with "NO-TEA-SIR" you will have a blank at 3 and 7. In such case, the second row will carry the numbers 30 trough 39 and the third row 70 through 79. Again, which digits are used for a given character is unimportant and has absolutely no effect on the security of the message, as one-time pad encryption is applied. Many variations on this checkerboard are possible, as long as both sender and receiver agree on a common system.

The CT-37 table is an extended version of the straddling checkerboard and includes additional characters. The table is easy to remember. It uses the 7 most frequent English letters "ESTONIA" in the top row. The two following rows are the remaining letters, completed with the "FIG" field. The fourth row contains the "SPACE" and "CODE" field with the punctuation marks between them (less critical to remember).

Using the CT37 table is easy. All characters are encoded into their one-digit or two-digit value. To encode figures, always use "FIG" (89) just before and after figures. Each digit is written out three times to exclude errors. You can use spaces and punctuations within the "FIG" mode, for example, "1.5 KG" = "89 111 91 555 89 77 74 ". The "CODE" field is the optional codebook prefix.

E	S	T	O	N	I	A	CT - 37		
0	1	2	3	4	5	6			
B	C	D	F	G	H	J	K	L	M
70	71	72	73	74	75	76	77	78	79
P	Q	R	U	V	W	X	Y	Z	FIG
80	81	82	83	84	85	86	87	88	89
SPACE	(.)	(,)	(')	(?)	(/)	(+)	(-)	(=)	CODE
90	91	92	93	94	95	96	97	98	99

In this example we use the code 1234 at the end (which could, for instance, stand for "Send confirmation as soon as possible" in our codebook).

MEET ME AT "BRAVO" AT 1030 HR. SEND CONFIRMATION ASAP.

M E E T   M E   A T   ' B R A V O '
A T fi 1
79 0 0 2 90 79 0 90 6 2 90 93 70 82 6
84 3 93 6 2 89 111

0 3 0 fi H R . co 1234
000 333 000 89 75 82 91 99 1234

In groups:
79002 90790 90629 09370 82684 39362
89111 00033 30008 97582 91991 23400

The CT-37-words table uses a mix of letters, words and codes. CODE 6 is a shortened prefix for fixed length codes. The commonly used words "acknowledge", "request", "message", "rendez-vous point", "grid" (coordinates), "send" and "supply" are respresented by a small two-digit code. Omitting one more top-row letter or the CODE field will give another full row which could held 10 more words, expressions or short sentences (CODE could be added to this new row). This approach can reduce the message length enormously if the set of two-digit expressions is selected carfully.

A	E	I	N	O	T	CODE	CT-37 w		
0	1	2	3	4	5	6			
B	C	D	F	G	H	J	K	L	M
70	71	72	73	74	75	76	77	78	79
P	Q	R	S	U	V	W	X	Y	Z
80	81	82	83	84	85	86	87	88	89
SPACE	(.)	ACK	REQ	MSG	RV	GRID	SEND	SUPP	F/L
90	91	92	93	94	95	96	97	98	99
0	1	2	3	4	5	6	7	8	9
000	111	222	333	444	555	666	777	888	999

In the CT-46 conversion table, we can use four full rows since we have four unused digits in the top row. This conversion table is not that hard to memorize. In the first row the 6 most frequent letters AEINOR get the single digits. Each next row starts with the remaining digits 7, 8, 9 or 0. The second and third row are the remaining letters of the alphabet. The fourth row contains the SPC and CODE with the signs in between (less important to memorize). The fifth row are simply the numbers preceded by a 0.

A	E	I	N	O	R	CT - 46			
1	2	3	4	5	6				
B	C	D	F	G	H	J	K	L	M
70	71	72	73	74	75	76	77	78	79
P	Q	S	T	U	V	W	X	Y	Z
80	81	82	83	84	85	86	87	88	89
SPC	(.)	(,)	(:)	?	/	(	)	"	CODE
90	91	92	93	94	95	96	97	98	99
0	1	2	3	4	5	6	7	8	9
00	01	02	03	04	05	06	07	08	09

The CT-55 table has even more additional characters. L/F 89 is used to switch from Letters (yellow) to Figures (green) and from Figures to Letters. This enables more characters with the same conversion value. The Red fields can be used in both Letters and Figures mode, thus a space, period, etc in a text doesn't require switching to Figures. Numbers are represented by its double code to exclude digit errors. An example: F-16B is converted to 73 89 84 11 66 89 70. CODE is again used as a prefix for four-digit codes and RPT is used to repeat important pieces of text. This conversion table has the 7 most frequent letters, optimized for English, and is suitable for text with more figures and signs.

A	E	I	N	O	S	T	CT-55		
0	1	2	3	4	5	6			
B	C	D	F	G	H	J	K	L	M
70	71	72	73	74	75	76	77	78	79
P	Q	R	U	V	W	X	Y	Z	L|F
80	81	82	83	84	85	86	87	88	89
SPC	CODE	RPT	(.)	(,)	(')	(:)	(	)	
90	91	92	93	94	95	96	97	98	
?	!	/	+	−	×	=			
80	81	82	83	84	85	86	87		89
0	1	2	3	4	5	6	7	8	9
00	11	22	33	44	55	66	77	88	99

Of course, there are many other ways to convert characters into numbers. The system of converting characters into digits doesn't need to be secure because the one-time pad provides the security. Any method to convert into digits is good, as long as it is practical, doesn't make the ciphertext too long and isn't prone to critical errors. More conversion tables and manual encryption methods, used by Intelligence agencies, are found on the SAS und Chiffrierdienst website

(c) Copyright 2004 - 2012 Dirk Rijmenants

###

Made in the USA
San Bernardino, CA
18 September 2016